RYAN MCDERMOTT

UNBOUND

Experiencing Life &
Freedom in Christ

Publishing Team

Content Editor
Kyle Wiltshire

Director, Student Ministry
Ben Trueblood

Production Editor
Morgan Hawk

Manager, Student Ministry Publishing
John Paul Basham

Graphic Designer
Shiloh Stufflebeam

Editorial Team Leader
Karen Daniel

Published by Lifeway Press®
©2022 Ryan McDermott

ISBN 978-1-0877-7349-0
Item 005839416
Dewey Decimal Classification Number: 230
Subject Heading: RELIGION / CHRISTIAN MINISTRY / YOUTH

Printed in the United States of America.

Student Ministry Publishing
Lifeway Resources
200 Powell Place, Suite 100
Brentwood, TN 37027

We believe that the Bible has God for its author; salvation for its end; and truth, without any mixture of error, for its matter and that all Scripture is totally true and trustworthy. To review Lifeway's doctrinal guideline, please visit www.lifeway.com/doctrinalguideline.

Unless otherwise noted, all Scripture quotations are taken from the Christian Standard Bible®, Copyright © 2017 by Holman Bible Publishers. Used by permission. Christian Standard Bible® and CSB® are federally registered trademarks of Holman Bible Publishers. Scripture quotations marked (ESV) are from the ESV® Bible (The Holy Bible, English Standard Version®), copyright © 2001 by Crossway, a publishing ministry of Good News Publishers. Used by permission. All rights reserved. Scripture quotations marked (NLT) are taken from the Holy Bible, New Living Translation, copyright ©1996, 2004, 2007, 2013, 2015 by Tyndale House Foundation. Used by permission of Tyndale House Publishers, Inc., Carol Stream, IL 60188. All rights reserved. Scripture quotations marked (KJV) are from the Holy Bible, King James Version.

CONTENTS

ABOUT THE AUTHOR

Ryan is passionate about preaching the gospel of Jesus, helping students be brave enough to believe they can change the world, and training the next generation of church leaders. He has an undergraduate degree in Christian Leadership from Palm Beach Atlantic University and a Master's degree in Ministerial Leadership from Southeastern University. Ryan has over seventeen years of experience serving students in the local church. Currently, he serves as the Executive Director of Family Ministry at Christ Fellowship Church, a non-denominational multi-site church with locations all across South Florida. Ryan lives in West Palm Beach, Florida, with his wife Christine and their two children, Declan and Kinley.

How To Use

This Bible study book includes six sessions of content. Each session includes video teaching, followed by content designed for groups and individuals.

WATCH GUIDE

Each teaching video is 6-8 minutes long and is designed to help students think about the topic for the session and engage in discussion. There is a guide with space for students to take notes as they watch the video teaching. Video content can be found at lifeway.com/unbound.

GROUP DISCUSSION

These pages include icebreakers, questions, activities, and statements that guide students to respond to the video teaching and to relevant Bible passages. It's important to consider the age, maturity level, and needs of students as you tailor this content for your group.

PERSONAL STUDY

Three days of personal study are provided for each session (except for session 6) to take students deeper into Scripture and to supplement the biblical truths introduced in the group discussion and teaching time. These pages challenge students to grow in their understanding of God's Word and to make practical applications to their lives.

LEADER GUIDE

At the back of the book is a leader guide to help walk students through the content. There you will find a summary of the discussion guide for each session.

SESSION 1:

WHEN JESUS SHOWS UP

WHEN JESUS
SHOWS UP,
DEAD THINGS
COME TO LIFE.

WATCH GUIDE

Key Scripture:

Jesus told her, "I am the resurrection and the life. Anyone who believes in me will live, even after dying" (John 11:25, NLT).

NOTES

GREAT QUOTE

KEY POINTS

GROUP DISCUSSION

ICEBREAKER

Begin by making sure everyone in the group knows each other. Ask each student to introduce themselves, then begin the activity.

Think of a moment that the students in your group would all be familiar with. Maybe a recent sporting event or story from summer camp that most, if not all, would have experienced. Then ask a student who witnessed the event to explain what happened. After allow another student to detail any differences in what they remember from the first account.

If time permits, allow someone who wasn't there to recap what they heard happened. It's probable there will be discrepancies between the eyewitness accounts and the ones who only heard what happened after.

DEBRIEF: The point of this icebreaker is to help students understand that the best perspective comes from those who saw something for themselves.

> ⁇ **QUESTION: Why are eyewitness accounts of an event often different from the retelling of someone who just heard about what happened?**

GROUP DISCUSSION

The Gospel of John is believed by many to be an eyewitness account by one of Jesus's disciples. He also happened to be one of Jesus's closest friends, which means we can be sure that it is accurate and trustworthy when we read the words of John.[1] Why? Because John was actually there. He saw these events with his very own eyes, and he wrote them down so that so that anyone who reads his words might "believe that Jesus is the Messiah, the Son of God, and that by believing [they] may have life in his name" (John 20:31).

ASK A VOLUNTEER TO READ JOHN 11:1-8.

The stories in the Gospel of John all follow a similar pattern. Jesus performs a miracle or makes a claim about Himself, which results in misunderstanding or controversy, and at the end of each story, people are forced to make a decision about who they believe Jesus is. The story of Lazarus represents a turning point in the Gospel of John. After this particular miracle, the conflict surrounding Jesus was so intense that religious leaders started plotting to kill Him, and they began to move forward with their murderous plan against Him (see John 11:53). When Jesus decided to go to Bethany, the disciples tried to talk Him out of it, but despite their very valid concerns for His life, Jesus went. It should strike us as incredibly significant that the turning point in the Gospel of John is not just a story about someone being brought back to life, but a story about Jesus willingly laying down His life for His friend.

> **② QUESTION: What are some of the claims about Jesus that people find controversial today?**

Throughout the Gospel of John, Jesus made a series of seven incredibly significant statements intended to define who He is. These claims of Jesus are so direct and personal that they all start with the phrase "I am." This phrase may not carry much significance for us, but Jewish people living at the time of Jesus would have understood each of these statements to be a claim that Jesus was, Himself, God. The "I am" statements of Jesus recorded in the Gospel of John would have reminded His original audience of an encounter that Moses had with God. Jesus's intentional use of the same phrase "draws on Exodus 3:14 and other Old Testament passages where the phrase clearly refers to God."[2] That is the very reason we see people get so upset with Jesus using this phrase. The statements He made were confusing, controversial, and offensive to some only because He claimed to be God.[3]

ACTIVITY

Take the next few minutes to search the Scriptures in the Gospel of John and examine the claims that Jesus made about Himself.

In John 6:35, Jesus said, "I am_____."

In John 8:12, Jesus said, "I am_____."

In John 10:9, Jesus said, "I am_____."

In John 10:14-15, Jesus said, "I am_____."

In John 11:25, Jesus said, "I am_____."

In John 14:6, Jesus said, "I am_____."

In John 15:5, Jesus said, "I am_____."

> ⑦ **QUESTION: What insights do you glean about Jesus from these seven "I am" statements?**

The "I am" statement in the story of Lazarus is found not in a conversation that Jesus had with Lazarus but with one of his sisters, Martha. She cried out to Jesus, expressing her frustration and making the desperate statement: "Lord, if you had been here, my brother wouldn't have died" (John 11:21). To which Jesus simply replied, "Your brother will rise again" (John 11:23). Martha's mind immediately went to a day in the future when she would be reunited with her brother; the last day when all will be raised again. Jesus, however, offered her not just a future hope but a present hope. Jesus said to her, "I am the resurrection and the life. The one who believes in me, even if he dies, will live" (John 11:25). And then? The demonstration. Jesus put on display for all to see His power over disease, death, and the grave. He revealed to those witnesses that there is a resurrection power in Him that is available in this life and the next.

God wants us to understand that the resurrection power of Jesus is not for somewhere, someday; it is for right here, right now. God wants us to understand that when Jesus shows up, dead things come to life. Thanks be to God, there is nothing too dead for Jesus! There is no situation, or circumstance, or individual that cannot experience the resurrection power of Jesus. When we invite God into the dark, desperate, broken, dead places in our lives, He brings His resurrection power to each and every one. God can breathe new life into our families, into our dreams, into our relationships, and even into us! This same God who raised Lazarus from the dead is available to anyone at any time.

QUESTION: Is there an area of your life that you need Jesus to breathe new life into today?

CLOSING PRAYER: Thank You, Jesus, for Your resurrection power in our lives. Help us to live in that power, knowing You bring dead things to life. Amen.

Jesus Is Never Late

(?) **Describe a time when you found it difficult to wait on something.**

Part of this story from the Gospel of John is about waiting. After presenting their problem to Jesus, Mary and Martha had to wait for a solution. When Jesus heard about Lazarus, He didn't drop everything and rush right to his side (see John 11:6). He didn't provide instant healing. He didn't tell the messengers, "Go; let it be done for you as you have believed," as He did in Matthew 8:13 (ESV). Not this time. He simply sent back a promise, "This sickness will not end in death but is for the glory of God, so that the Son of God may be glorified through it" (John 11:4). Lazarus's sickness not only persisted, it progressed. He got even sicker and eventually died. It wasn't until he had been in the tomb for four days that Jesus finally showed up.

(?) **When have you waited for God to respond after desperately asking Him for something?**

Why did Jesus make them wait? John 11:5-6 seem to give us at least one reason: "Now Jesus loved Martha, her sister, and Lazarus. So when he heard that he was sick, he stayed two more days in the place where he was." To say it another way, Jesus loved them, so He stayed where He was. Wait, what? The text seems to suggest that His love for them is one of the reasons He made them wait. His love for them was one of His motivations for *not* snapping His fingers and making their problem disappear.

What if God is making us wait because He loves us? What if we actually began to believe that when God makes us wait, it is not because He is withholding something from us or because He is punishing us, but because of His infinite love for us? I wonder how that would change our perspective on "unanswered" prayers or unrealized dreams. I wonder how that would change how we wait upon the Lord.

(?) Have you ever had a time when God made you wait on something, and the result was so much better than you imagined? Describe it here.

Charles Spurgeon, often referred to as the "Prince of Preachers,"[4] once wrote: "Remember this, had any other condition been better for you than the one in which you are, divine love would have put you there."[5] In moments of hardship, trial, difficulty, or persecution, we need to remember that while our position might seem otherwise, God will sometimes allow us to struggle *because* He loves us.

We see in this story that Jesus is never late. He delays in coming so God would be glorified in their situation. He arrives at just the right moment so that everyone would know: Jesus truly is the Son of God. Prior to the coming of Christ, miracles were divided into two categories according to Jewish tradition: those that anyone could perform if empowered to do so, and those reserved only for the Messiah.[6] This was one of those "Messiah Only" miracles. Not simply because Jesus raised a man from the dead, but it is the timing that makes this miracle so significant. When did Jesus arrive? On the fourth day. Rabbis taught that it was possible for someone to return from the dead if done within three days.[7] They believed that the spirit of a person would hover around the dead body for three days after death, but after those three days, the spirit would depart and returning from the dead was no longer possible.

When Jesus raised Lazarus on the fourth day, He was clearly demonstrating His power over death and the grave, but also over time and expectation. Despite how we might sometimes feel, Jesus is never late, and He always has the power to change everything.

(?) Is there an area of your life in which you need to trust God's timing today? Write about it below.

PRAY: Lord Jesus, help me understand today that waiting is not a waste when I am waiting on You. Help me to trust Your timing in every area of my life today. Amen.

Jesus Is Never Surprised

(?) **Where do you turn in times of trouble?**

(?) **Do you present your problems to Jesus?**

(?) **Is that normally your first reaction or your last resort?**

I love that Mary and Martha turned to Jesus with their problem. I don't know if it was their first reaction or a last resort, but either way, they brought their problem to the only person who could do something about it. Jesus cares about the details of our lives, and He longs to hear from us. We should not assume that Jesus was unaware that Lazarus was sick until He got the message from Mary and Martha. In fact, the opposite is true. Jesus knows all of our needs, desires, and problems before we do. Praying to Jesus and presenting our problems to Him is not for His awareness but for our relationship. He longs for us to come to Him in prayer, for us to declare our dependence on Him, for us to invite Him to involve Himself in our situation. Good fathers love to hear from their kids. God doesn't need you to inform Him about the details of your life, but He desires a relationship with you. When we pray, according to Psalm 116, God bends down to listen. He turns His ear to hear.

WRITE: Look up these Scriptures, and list what each one reveals about God's knowledge of our lives.

Psalm 56:8	
Psalm 147:5	
Isaiah 40:28	
Matthew 10:30	
Romans 11:33	

It is important for us to realize that God has never been shocked. He has never been caught off-guard. Nothing has ever occurred to God. He knows. He is infinitely aware of the details of our lives. That fact should bring us great comfort because it means the things in life that we don't see coming and are not prepared for do not take God by surprise. When we feel alarmed or confused or shocked or uncertain, we can turn to a God who is absolutely none of those things. Psalm 139:1-6 (ESV), among many other places in Scripture, speaks to God being all-knowing. David wrote:

> *O Lord, you have searched me and known me! You know when I sit down and when I rise up; you discern my thoughts from afar. You search out my path and my lying down and are acquainted with all my ways. Even before a word is on my tongue, behold, O Lord, you know it altogether. You hem me in, behind and before, and lay your hand upon me. Such knowledge is too wonderful for me; it is high; I cannot attain it.*

So whether you are presenting a problem to God or confessing your sin, you cannot shock or surprise Him. He just wants to hear it from you. Whenever I got in trouble as a kid, the hardest part was always waiting for my dad to come home. I knew that when he got there, I would have to explain to him what I had done. Of course, he already knew. There was no doubt in my mind that my mom had already filled him in but hearing it directly from me carried a different weight. Good fathers love to hear from their children. God is already infinitely aware of the details of our lives, but He also chooses to be intimately involved with us. The more we communicate with God, the stronger our relationship with Him will be.

(?) **Is there something you are facing right now that you have been hesitant to bring to the Lord? What is it?**

PRAY: Lord Jesus, I thank You that I can always turn to You no matter what it is that I am facing. Thank You for hearing my cries. Help me to trust You with my problems today. Amen.

Jesus Weeps

Upon arriving at Bethany, Jesus found an entire community had surrounded Mary and Martha in their grief over Lazarus's death. Both sisters said the same thing to Jesus, "Lord, if you had been here, my brother would not have died" (John 11:21,32, ESV). The Bible tells us that when Jesus heard this and saw the mourning of the people, "he was deeply moved in his spirit and troubled" (John 11:33, ESV). So much so that when they showed Jesus the tomb Lazarus has been buried in, He sat down and began to cry. Let's just make sure we understand what happened here: God cried. The same God who breathed the stars into existence. The same God who set the sun in its place and the earth on its axis. The same God, who formed man from the dust of the ground and puts breath in your lungs, cried.

(?) Have you ever shared in someone's grief or walked alongside someone who was having a hard time? Describe it.

Jesus shared in their sorrow over death. Why would He do this? We know how this story ends—He raises Lazarus from the dead. Just a few seconds later, these people witness a miracle and are reunited with the one they love, and Jesus was the only one who knew what was about to happen. It is so significant that Jesus didn't tell them to stop wailing, crying, and grieving. Instead, He sat down outside the grave of His friend and cried. It may be the shortest verse in the Bible, but it is arguably one of the most significant, "Jesus wept" (John 11:35).

There were a few reasons for Jesus's tears. One reason is because His people were weeping. Psalm 34:18 tells us: "The Lord is near the brokenhearted; he saves those crushed in spirit." In Matthew 5:4, Jesus Himself proclaimed, "Blessed are those who mourn, for they will be comforted." In the story of Lazarus, we see Jesus putting these promises into action. He joined with those who were broken-hearted. He mourned with those who were mourning and wept with those who were weeping. Why does that matter? Because it means you are not alone when you grieve. You are not alone when you cry. You are not alone when you are broken-hearted. In those moments, Jesus does not tell us to suck it up, get tough, or move on. Instead, He sits with us, has compassion for us, mourns with us, and grieves with us. Psalm 46:1 tells us that God is our ever-present help in times of need. When we face difficulty in life we may feel—perhaps more than ever—that Jesus is close.

(?) Do you have Scriptures you cling to in moments of difficulty? What are they and why are they important to you?

I believe Jesus also wept here over the state of creation. Death was never meant to exist in the world that God created. It wasn't a part of His original design. When Adam and Eve disobeyed God in the garden of Eden, sin entered the world and with it shame, pain, grief, sorrow, evil, disease, and death (see Gen. 3). None of which were meant for God's people. What does that mean for us? Even though we have the opportunity to enjoy eternal life through a relationship with Jesus, God is still grieved by the things we must endure because of our fallen world.

I also think Jesus was sad. Hebrews 4:15 explains that Jesus was human, just like us. Therefore, He understands what we go through. He has felt everything that we feel. Here is what you have to understand about Jesus: He was 100 percent man and 100 percent God. He is the only 200 percent being to ever exist. In this story, we see the full humanity and the full divinity of Jesus on display. The man who wept over the death of His friend is the same God who called him forth from the grave. It's okay to feel sad sometimes. Emotions are not bad. Our emotions, however, must be connected to and informed by a greater reality. In 1 Thessalonians 4:13, Paul told the church that unless we set our sights on the reality of resurrection, we will continue to grieve as those who have no hope. What is his point? The fact that Jesus is alive and resurrection from the dead is possible through Him changes the way we view everything. It offers us hope in the midst of life's most difficult moments. This life is fleeting and temporary and fading, but there is a day coming when Jesus will right every wrong, heal every wound, and dry every tear.

(?) Read 2 Corinthians 4:13–18. How does this passage of Scripture connect to the concepts we have just discussed?

PRAY: Lord Jesus, thank You for being a God who weeps and thank You for being a God who comforts. Today, help me to understand how Your resurrection power changes everything. Amen.

SESSION 2:

DO YOU BELIEVE?

IT'S POSSIBLE FOR YOU TO EXPERIENCE RESURRECTION LIFE. IT'S POSSIBLE FOR YOU TO BE ALIVE IN CHRIST. BUT HERE'S THE REAL QUESTION: DO YOU BELIEVE THIS? BECAUSE IF YOU DO, YOU TOO CAN BE SAVED.

WATCH GUIDE

Key Scripture:

"Everyone who lives and believes in me will never die. Do you believe this?" (John 11:26, ESV).

NOTES

GREAT QUOTE

KEY POINTS

GROUP DISCUSSION

ICEBREAKER

Play a game called "Do you believe this?" in which students identify whether they believe something to be true or false. If they believe it, direct them to stand. If they do not, ask students to stay seated.

1. Toilet seats are the dirtiest objects in your house, do you believe this? A: It's false. Toilet seats have ten times fewer germs than cell phones.[1]

2. There is a tree in India that has a root system larger than the average Walmart, do you believe this? A: It's true. There is a 250-year-old Great Banyan tree that has aerial roots covering 3.5 square acres of land.[2]

3. Humans have only five senses, do you believe this? A: It's false. There are at least nine (depending on your definition) including our ability to feel the passing of time and sense of balance.[3]

4. There was a man who received the highest military honor from both the Allies and Axis Powers in World War II, do you believe this? A: It's true. His name was Juan Pujol Garcia, and he was a Spanish spy working as a double agent for both sides.[4]

Feel free to add more questions if you would like to extend the game.

RECAP

In Session 1, we barely began to scratch the surface of all that God has to teach us through this story in John 11. We listened to and, hopefully, felt the story of Lazarus in a fresh new way. Now that we know the story, we have to ask ourselves if we understand the story. What really is the point of this passage? What does it mean for you and me today? Is this just Lazarus's story, or could it be more?

GROUP DISCUSSION

ASK FOR A VOLUNTEER TO READ JOHN 11:17-27.
In these verses is a question we all must answer. Leaders, take time to share your personal salvation story. Talk about the moment when you came to believe that Jesus is the resurrection and life. Include elements of your life before Jesus and what has happened since you have become a Christ-follower.

ACTIVITY

There came a point in my life when I realized that I had to commit to Jesus with my whole heart. I had to believe. How about you? Ask students to read aloud the following Scriptures about salvation and eternal life.

John 1:12
"But to all who did receive [Jesus], he gave them the right to be children of God, to those who believe in his name."

John 3:16
"For God loved the world in this way: He gave his one and only Son, so that everyone who believes in him will not perish but have eternal life."

Acts 4:12
"There is salvation in no one else, for there is no other name under heaven given to people by which we must be saved."

⑦ **QUESTION: What similarities do you find among these three verses?**

⑦ **QUESTION: Is each verse basically saying the same thing? If so, what are they saying?**

⑦ **QUESTION: Do you believe this?**

ACTIVITY

We must all come to that place of belief and confession like Martha (see John 11:27). Most of you have come to that point of belief. Take some time to write out the story of when you first placed your faith in Jesus.

Answer these questions to tell your story of belief.

What was your life like before Jesus?

_____
_____
_____
_____

Who introduced you to Jesus?

_____
_____

What lead you to the point of believing in Jesus?

_____
_____
_____
_____
_____

What has your life been like since you have placed your faith in Jesus?

_____
_____
_____
_____
_____

Note to Leaders: There may be students in your group who have not placed their faith in Jesus. If this is the case, use the following to help guide you through a conversation with them.

Use this outline to explain the gospel:

God's Love: God revealed His love for us most clearly in the person of Jesus (John 3:16).

Our Sin: We have all sinned and need forgiveness (Rom. 3:23).

God's Gift: Yes, we have sinned, but God provided eternal life for us through Jesus (Rom. 6:23).

My Confession: Each one of us must confess Jesus as the Lord of our lives (Rom. 10:9-10).

If you've never experienced that moment before, today can be the day when you cross from death to life. If you would like to make that decision, pray this prayer with me.

Pray: "Lord Jesus, I need You. Come into my life. Make me new again. I give You my sin, and I receive the eternal life You purchased for me on the cross and sealed for me when You rose again three days later. For the rest of my days, through the power of the Holy Spirit in me, I will live to honor You. Amen!"

There is nothing magical about those words, but there is something deeply spiritual. In that moment, the old is gone and the new has come. Your sin has been separated from you as far as the east is from the west, and you are adopted into the family of God forever. All of heaven celebrates that decision with you today! Now you have something to write about. Get to it!

ACTIVITY

Now that students have written it down, have each person take a few minutes telling the story of when they first placed their faith in Jesus.

CLOSING PRAYER: Jesus, we are grateful that only You have the power to bring the dead to life. Help us to see You through this study. Amen.

You Only Die Once

I have no doubt you have probably heard the word "YOLO" before, but just so we are on the same page, it's a goofy acronym that stands for "you only live once." By and large, it was used as an encouragement to live in the moment, do whatever you want, and give little thought to the future or the consequences of your actions. The story of Lazarus kind of messes with this phrase though, doesn't it? He got to live twice, right? He got another chance at life after being physically brought back from the dead. I would imagine he took the opportunity to cross a few more items off his bucket list or extend a few long overdue apologies. I don't actually know what he did, but I would imagine he probably lived differently the second time around.

(?) What would you change about your life if you got a second chance at living?

Even though Lazarus got a second chance at life, what is perhaps more important is that he got a second chance at death. I think that is the real gift in this story. In John 11, Jesus only restored physical life to Lazarus temporarily. There eventually came a day when he would die again. Lazarus was given another opportunity to prepare for that day. This is incredibly important, especially when we consider the claim Jesus made in John 11:25, "I am the resurrection and the life. The one who believes in me, even if he dies, will live. Everyone who lives and believes in me will never die." The only thing that would allow Lazarus to live beyond the day of his (next) death was belief in Jesus. The temporary second-chance at physical life he had been granted was nothing compared to the eternal spiritual life Jesus desired to give him. Lazarus, just like Mary and Martha, and just like you and me, had to confess Jesus Christ as Lord and believe that God had raised him from the dead if he wanted to be saved and receive eternal life.

(?) What should you change about your life knowing that you only get one chance at dying?

When I was young, we used to visit my great grandmother often. We called her Nanny, and I really loved going to see her. Her room always smelled of ripe bananas. Kind of weird, I know. She had this big banana tree outside her front door, and she would always cut them off and have a big bowl of bananas on the table to share with anyone who came to visit. To this day, anytime I smell a banana I still think of her. Nanny was the first person I loved who passed away, and I remember hearing this story of Lazarus around the time of her passing. The words of Jesus and the promise of the resurrection and life after death gave me so much hope. I knew that my Nanny had confessed Jesus as Lord, and since she believed in him, she was not actually dead but was fully alive with Jesus. It gives me so much hope to know that the people around me—those I love and care about—will never die if they trust in Jesus for salvation.

ACTIVITY: Choose one (or more) of the following Scriptures about eternal life to begin memorizing today.

John 3:16

John 17:3

Romans 6:23

1 John 5:11-12

PRAY: Lord Jesus, thank You for life after death. Thank You for the hope I have in the resurrection. May I live my temporary physical life ever mindful of the more important eternal spiritual life that is to come. Amen.

Yes, No, or Not Yet

(?) **Describe a time when you felt like God did not answer your prayer *or* when you felt like God did not answer your prayer in the way that you expected Him to.**

I can recall several times in my life when I prayed for something specific, and it felt like my prayers went unanswered. I've prayed for opportunities that never came about. I've prayed for grades that I never received. I've prayed for relationships that haven't yet been restored, and I've even prayed for healing that did not come. It can be easy in those moments to feel some frustration toward God for not answering our prayers or for not answering them how we expected He would. Whenever there is a gap between our expectation and our experience, frustration, disappointment, doubt, and even anger can creep in. In part, that is what we see happen to Mary and Martha in John 11. They presented their problem to Jesus (much like we do in prayer) and expected Him to come immediately and heal their brother Lazarus. But He didn't. Now what?

(?) **What emotions do you see Mary and Martha display in John 11:17–32? How do you think you might have felt if you were in their shoes?**

John 11:20 paints an interesting picture: "As soon as Martha heard that Jesus was coming, she went to meet him, but Mary remained seated in the house." We see one person who was ready to have a conversation with Jesus and another who would rather just stay where she was. These are two very different reactions. One sister was eager to confront Jesus and her feelings, and the other would prefer to keep to herself and sit in her sorrow. I think it is important when we experience disappointment, frustration, doubt, and even anger to bring those emotions to Jesus. He can handle it. I love that Jesus doesn't rebuke Martha for what she said to Him or even how she said it. He didn't scold her for being upset. He embraced her emotions and He pointed her to a greater hope that has yet to come. Because Martha was willing to have a conversation, even when she was so clearly upset, Jesus could remind her of the truth and the promise of eternal life.

(?) **When there is a gap between your expectation and experience, do you find it easy to talk to God? Why or why not?**

I believe that God always answers prayer. We do have to prepare ourselves, though, because God may not always answer them in the way we want. This may seem simplistic, but I believe that God's three responses to our prayers can usually be reduced to "yes," "no," or "not yet." When God says "yes," it is because the prayers we have prayed align with His will, and He is delighted to accommodate the requests of His children and give us the desires of our hearts. When God says "no," we can trust that it is because it is not for our ultimate good. Isaiah 55:8-9 reminds us that His ways and thoughts are higher than ours. Romans 8:28 tells us that God is working all things together for the good of those who love Him and are called according to His purpose. If God says "no," it is because He has something better for us. When God says "not yet," it is like a good parent telling a seven-year-old that they can't drive a car: we will get there one day, but if that request were granted now, it could have devastating consequences.

(?) **What are some other truths from God's Word you should remind yourself of when it feels like your prayers have not been answered or have not been answered in the way you expected?**

PRAY: Lord Jesus, thank You for being a God who longs to give us the desire of our hearts, but thank You for being a God who loves us enough to sometimes say "no." Help me to trust Your ways and Your timing for my life. Amen.

Mary and Martha Moments

John 11 isn't the only time we see Jesus with these two sisters in the Bible. There are two other occasions when Mary and Martha were together that are recorded in the Gospels. One of these moments is found in Luke 10 and would have taken place before the raising of Lazarus. Another is in John 12 and would have taken place after Lazarus had been brought back to life. Each of these teach us some incredibly valuable lessons. Let's look at them in order. The first is when Jesus initially met these two women.

READ LUKE 10:38-42 IN YOUR BIBLE.

(?) **What are some observations you make about the relationship between Jesus, Mary, and Martha in this story?**

It's not hard to picture, right? Maybe you've become frustrated with a sibling for not helping you with your chores, or you've gotten upset with someone for not pulling their weight on a school project. When it feels like you are doing all the work, it is easy to feel like Martha did. Jesus lovingly corrected her, not for serving, but for being worried and upset. She was doing a good thing by working hard to take care of her special guests, but she was doing it in the wrong way. Mary used this moment as an opportunity to sit at the feet of Jesus, to take in His teaching, and to be in His presence. This story makes me wonder how many times I have missed out on what Jesus wanted to show me or teach me because I was too busy. Mary *believed* that spending time with Jesus was the most important thing she could ever do.

(?) **Do you value time with Jesus above all else? What are some of the things that distract you from time with Him? How can you prioritize sitting at Jesus's feet?**

The second story took place not long after the miracle recorded in John 11.

READ JOHN 12:1-8 IN YOUR BIBLE.

(?) **What are some similarities you see between this story and Luke 10:38-42?**

They obviously had much to celebrate. This was like a party in honor of what Jesus did for their family. Lazarus was sitting and eating with Jesus, which is even more proof that the man who was once dead was now alive. Martha was showing her gratitude for Jesus by serving and making all of the arrangements. Mary, looking for some way to show her devotion, admiration, and love for Jesus, anointed Him with a very expensive collection of perfume (likely equivalent to a year's wages).[5] Normally, an anointing like this would have been poured over the head, but Mary, longing to express a deep gratitude, went beyond the tradition and anointed Jesus's feet.[6] Because of who Jesus was and what He had done for them, Mary and Martha offered Jesus their time, their talents, and their treasure.

(?) **What can you offer to Jesus today as an expression of your love and gratitude?**

PRAY: Lord Jesus, help me each and every day to give my time, talents, and treasure in response to who You are and what You have done for me. Amen.

SESSION 3:

GRAVE CLOTHES

YOU MIGHT
BE BOUND,
BUT YOU DON'T
HAVE TO BE.
JESUS, BY THE
POWER OF HIS
RESURRECTION,
CALLS US TO
LIFE AND
FREEDOM.

WATCH GUIDE

Key Scripture:

The dead man came out, his hands and feet wrapped with strips of linen, and a cloth around his face (John 11:44, NIV).

NOTES

GREAT QUOTE

KEY POINTS

GROUP DISCUSSION

ICEBREAKER

Ask students to get into groups of two to four people. Give each group a roll of toilet paper, and challenge them to wrap the entire roll of toilet paper around one group member in sixty seconds. Call time and make sure they stay wrapped up as you compare each group's final result. After you have identified the winning group, then have students escape from the toilet paper that binds them as quickly as they can.

RECAP

In the last session, we talked about our belief in Jesus and shared our stories of how we came to faith in Him. Can you imagine the story Lazarus had to tell? Let's read back over his story so it's fresh and clear in our minds as we discuss what we've just watched.

ASK FOR A VOLUNTEER TO READ JOHN 11:38-44.

GROUP DISCUSSION

Most of us probably envisioned Lazarus running from the grave after Jesus called him out, but there would be no way for this to happen due to his grave clothes.

> **② QUESTION: What images come to mind when you envision the story of Lazarus begin brought back to life from the grave?**

The grave clothes that bound Lazarus after Jesus called him back from the dead is a perfect picture of how many of us are living. We have answered "Yes" will full confidence to the question Jesus asked in John 11:26, "Do you believe this?" But many believers are still bound like Lazarus. We're stuck in our grave clothes. To understand why this is, it would be helpful to turn our attention all the way back to the book of Genesis, the first book of the Bible.

Right from the beginning, we see the power and creativity of God on display as He spoke all of creation into existence. With His words, God created light, He called the mountains to emerge from the ground, He hung the stars in the sky, and He populated the planet with living plants and animals. Then God said,

"Let us make man in our image, according to our likeness. They will rule the fish of the sea, the birds of the sky, the livestock, the whole earth, and the creatures that crawl on the earth." So God created man in his own image; he created him in the image of God; he created them male and female.

Genesis 1:26–27

? QUESTION: What sets humans apart from the rest of creation?

Humanity is distinct from the rest of creation in several very important ways. First, we were made in the image of God. We are meant to be walking, talking, reflections of our Creator. Second, we were given dominion over everything else that God created. Third, we were built different.

Then the LORD God formed the man out of the dust from the ground and breathed the breath of life into his nostrils, and the man became a living being.

Genesis 2:7

You see, while the world was formed by God's words, Adam and Eve were handcrafted. Scripture says that they were formed from the dust of the ground. Human beings were the first thing in Scripture that God touched. Not only that but humans were filled with God's breath. This is important because we need to understand that humanity, including you and me, was made in the image of God by the hand of God and filled with the breath of God.

? QUESTION: How does understanding that humans—you and me— were made in the image of God, by the hand of God, and filled with the breath of God, shape your view of people? How does it shape your view of yourself?

Up to this point, everything sounds great. Although this story is incredibly good, something goes terribly wrong. God gave one command to Adam, "You are free to eat from any tree of the garden, but you must not eat from the tree of the knowledge of good and evil, for on the day you eat from it, you will certainly die" (Gen. 2:16-17). In the very next chapter, Satan slithered his ugly little head into this story and tempted Eve.

"Now the serpent was the most cunning of all the wild animals that the Lord God had made. He said to the woman, "Did God really say, 'You can't eat from any tree in the garden'?"
Genesis 3:1

Those four words, "Did God really say?" changed the trajectory of history forever. They are the same words Satan still uses to this day. His primary objective is to get you to question what God has said and who He has created you to be.

? QUESTION: How have you seen or experienced Satan saying, "Did God really say?"

Eve responded, "We may eat the fruit from the trees in the garden. But about the fruit of the tree in the middle of the garden, God said, 'You must not eat it or touch it, or you will die'" (Gen. 3:2). Notice here that Eve misquoted God. God said nothing about touching it. Only that they couldn't eat from it. Why did Eve misquote God? She did not know the word of God for herself; she had only heard it from Adam.

Here is a harsh reality: Many Christians misquote God today because they don't know His Word for themselves. They've heard it from a parent or a friend or a pastor, but when Satan slithers up and asks, "Did God really say?" the best answer they can offer is "I don't know." If we expect to resist the attacks of the enemy we have to know God's Word for ourselves.

? QUESTION: How does knowing God's Word for yourself help you fend off attacks from Satan?

Eve fell for Satan's trick. She ate the fruit and gave some to Adam, and he ate it too. With that act of disobedience, sin and brokenness entered the world. No longer did Adam and Eve enjoy a perfect relationship with God, His creation, and with each other, but now they experienced the consequences for their sin—consequences that are still being felt to this day.

After they ate the fruit, the Bible says, "Then the eyes of both of them were opened, and they knew they were naked; so they sewed fig leaves together and made coverings for themselves" (Gen. 3:7).

As a result of sin, Adam and Eve experienced shame and fear and they hid from God. These fig leaves they sewed to cover themselves up were the very first "grave clothes" we see in Scripture. Grave clothes are anything that holds us back from everything God has for us. It was never God's intention that His people be bound. In fact, God's intention for His people is fullness and freedom. The very first words that God spoke over Adam were "You are free…" (Gen. 2:16). But they were in bondage because of their sin.

? QUESTION: How do you describe the freedom you experience in Jesus to someone else?

This is our story, this is our problem. But thanks be to God, Jesus has made a way for us to be in right relationship with God again. He died a death that He did not deserve so that we might inherit a life we do not deserve. What was done in the garden can be undone through a relationship with Jesus. We can experience the fullness and freedom God intended in the beginning.

> *For since death came through a man, the resurrection*
> *of the dead also comes through a man. For just as in Adam*
> *all die, so also in Christ all will be made alive.*
> 1 Corinthians 15:21–22

We might be bound, but we don't have to be.

ACTIVITY

Give each student in your group a piece of paper of these Scriptures on the freedom we have in Jesus (John 8:36; Rom. 6:22; 2 Cor. 3:17; Gal. 5:1). Encourage students to memorize these verses and keep this physical sheet in their purse, backpack, or pocket. Remind students that Satan deceives us when we don't know the Word of God for ourselves. Memorizing the Word of God for ourselves and having it near will help us when we feel tempted.

CLOSING PRAYER: Lord, we don't want to be bound by sin. We want to live in the freedom You promised us. Help us to know Your Word and to use it to defend ourselves against the attacks of the enemy. Amen.

The Hurt We've Received

As you've already heard, grave clothes can represent *anything* that holds us back from *everything* God has for us. This week is all about understanding the grave clothes that we are wearing, so we can identify them, shed them, and walk in the freedom that only Jesus can give us.

One major thing that holds people back from walking in freedom and fullness is the pain of their past. Every person on planet Earth has experienced hurt, but our spiritual enemy tries to convince us that we are alone in our pain. He tries to tell us we are the only ones who have been through this or that no one else will understand. Sometimes he even uses guilt or shame to convince us that we should be embarrassed by our pain or that we are somehow at fault. So we keep everything to ourselves and fail to process our pain. Maybe you've never shared with anyone how you've been hurt. Maybe you've never talked about the pain that you are carrying. Keeping that a secret just allows the pain and the hurt to grow. We need to bring our pain into the light if we ever want to heal from it.

(?) **Is there pain from your past you haven't shared yet? What is it? What trusted adult can you share this pain with?**

It would be great if sharing our pain was the only step toward healing. It is the first step, but it is not the only step. Depending on the severity of the wound or the amount of time it has been there, it can take a long time to deal with the pain of our past. Some wounds, whether physical, emotional, or spiritual, take more work to heal than others. Don't be discouraged! Once you have shared it with someone, you are on the journey towards healing. One thing is certain: healing is not possible apart from forgiveness. God has actually designed it that way. It is not possible for us to walk in freedom and fullness without practicing forgiveness.

ACTIVITY: Look up the following verses on forgiveness and write each one out on a separate piece of paper:
Proverbs 17:9; Matthew 6:14; Mark 11:25; Luke 6:27; Luke 6:37; Romans 12:18; Colossians 3:13.

I've heard it said that refusing to forgive is like drinking poison and expecting the other person to die. By withholding forgiveness we are only hurting ourselves. It's easy to see from just the few Scriptures in the activity that forgiveness is a big deal to God, which means forgiveness ought to be a big deal for us. The best way to live a full and free life is to get very good at extending forgiveness. Obviously, this is easier said than done. As the Scriptures tell us, we should first be reminded of how much God has forgiven us; it then becomes easier to extend that same forgiveness to others. Contrary to popular opinion, forgiving does not mean forgetting. The goal is not to forget. That is unrealistic and unhelpful. But even in remembering the pain and what caused it, it is possible to choose forgiveness.

Laramiun Byrd was only twenty years old when he was shot and killed by sixteen-year-old Oshea Israel. Oshea was convicted of second-degree murder and sentenced to twenty-five years in prison. Eleven years after the trial, Mary Johnson, Laramiun's mother, decided to visit Oshea in prison. She realized she had not forgiven him and that unforgiveness was taking its toll on her. In their first meeting, Mary said that the Lord changed her heart and she was able to truly forgive Oshea. It became the first of many visits. When Oshea was released from prison in 2010, Mary not only threw a party for him, but she helped him secure a place to live—right next door to her. They have been neighbors ever since.

This story reminds me that forgiveness is possible. Even when it is not convenient, even when it doesn't make sense, even when it hurts—it is possible. Forgiveness is not just possible, it is beautiful, important, necessary, and inspiring.

(?) **Is there someone you have struggled to extend forgiveness to? Who is it? What step can you take today?**

PRAY: Lord Jesus, help me to see where I have held on to unforgiveness. Help me to forgive others as You have forgiven me. Amen.

The Lies We Believe

Another major thing that holds us back from walking in freedom and fullness is the lies we believe. Some lies can cut us so deeply and can derail our lives in serious ways. If you start to believe a lie like, "I'm not smart enough," "I'm not pretty enough," or "I'm not skinny enough," those lies can cost you everything. I grew up believing the lie that I had to perform and succeed for people to love me. When I became a Christian, I transferred that lie to my relationship with God. I thought if I worked harder, served more, or was somehow more perfect than everyone else, then God would love me more. It has taken me a long time to undo this lie and realize God's love for me is not based on my performance or success. God's love cannot be earned; it can only be received.

 **Fill in the blank: Sometimes I believe the lie that "I'm not _____ enough."**

The number one thing we can do to combat the lies we tend to believe is to immerse ourselves in the truth. Where do we find the truth? God's Word. We must read it, study it, and memorize it. It is easy to spot lies when we know the truth. God's Word is a weapon to combat the lies of the enemy.

You've probably seen a movie where a soldier is taking apart his weapon and reassembling it as fast as he possibly can. Why? Because a soldier must know their weapon inside and out. Why? Because when a problem comes up and his gun is jammed in the field, he must know how to fix it fast. Why? Because his life depends on it. Imagine if we knew Scripture that well? Imagine if we were so intimately acquainted with the Word of God that whenever something came up or something went wrong, we knew exactly where to go. God has given us a precious gift in His Word. Don't miss it. His Word is our weapon against lies.

(?) Can you name three things God's Word says are true about you?

The following are just a few things that God's Word says about you: You are a new creation (2 Cor. 5:17). You are accepted (Rom. 15:7). You are chosen (Eph. 1:4). You are forgiven (Rom. 8:1). You are loved (Rom. 8:39). You are a friend of Jesus (John 15:15). You are adopted into God's family (Eph. 2:19). This list barely even scratches the surface. There is so much more!

ACTIVITY: Circle any lie on this list that you tend to believe. Once you have identified a few that stick out to you, look up the corresponding truth from God's Word. Write the verse out. Keep it close and commit it to memory.

LIE	TRUTH FROM GOD'S WORD
I am unwanted.	1 John 3:1a
I am a mistake.	Psalm 139:13-16
I am unloved.	John 3:16
I am unlovable.	Jeremiah 31:3b
I am alone.	Psalm 27:10
I am not good enough.	Ephesians 2:10
I'll never be forgiven.	Ephesians 1:6-7
I'll never change.	2 Corinthians 5:17
I can't connect with God.	Hebrews 4:16

PRAY: Lord Jesus, help me to guard my heart and mind in You. Help me not to believe lies. Help me to choose the truth of Your Word. Amen.

The Sin We Can't Leave

This week is all about understanding what grave clothes we are wearing so that we can identify them, shed them, and walk in the freedom only Jesus can give us. Almost assuredly, the biggest obstacle to a life of freedom and fullness in Christ is our own sin. Therefore, it is important that we define the word "sin."

 How would you define sin?

According to Romans 3:23, sin can be understood as falling short of God's standards for our lives. Essentially, sin is anytime we miss the mark or disobey God. Sin is something we are all guilty of. Don't worry. It's not just you; it's me too. In 1 John 1:8, the Bible tells us, "If we say, 'We have no sin,' we are deceiving ourselves, and the truth is not in us." Thankfully, the very next verse tells us exactly what to do: "If we confess our sins, he is faithful and righteous to forgive us our sins and to cleanse us from all unrighteousness" (1 John 1:9).

So the first step to shedding the grave clothes of our sin is confession. In order to identify and confess our sins, it may be helpful to think about them in two different categories: **omission** and **commission.**

Sins of omission are when you *don't* do what you *should* do.

Sins of commission are when you *do* what you *should not* do.

(?) **Are there any sins of omission you need to confess? List them as an act of confession before the Lord.**

(?) Are there any sins of commission that you need to confess? List them as an act of confession before the Lord.

Once we confess our sins to the Lord, a very important step to be able to overcome those sins is confessing them to other people. We confess our sins to God as an act of repentance, turning away from our sin and turning back to God. We confess our sins to others as an act of accountability. This is the idea that we are open and transparent about our struggles with trusted, like-minded believers for the purpose of allowing them to ask us about how we are doing in this area of our lives (see James 5:16).

When accountability is at its best, you basically have to trip over those who hold you accountable if you try to return to the same sin. These conversations and relationships are for the purpose of helping us avoid sin as much as possible. When considering with whom to share your sin struggles, you should look for someone who loves Jesus, knows God's Word, is of the same gender, and if possible, is a little farther along on the journey of faith than you. This is an area where godly adult mentors can be a significant blessing.

(?) Is there someone who meets these qualifications that you can ask to hold you accountable for the sins you are trying to shed?

PRAY: Lord Jesus, help me to be open and honest about my sin with the right people so that I can experience freedom and fullness in You. Amen.

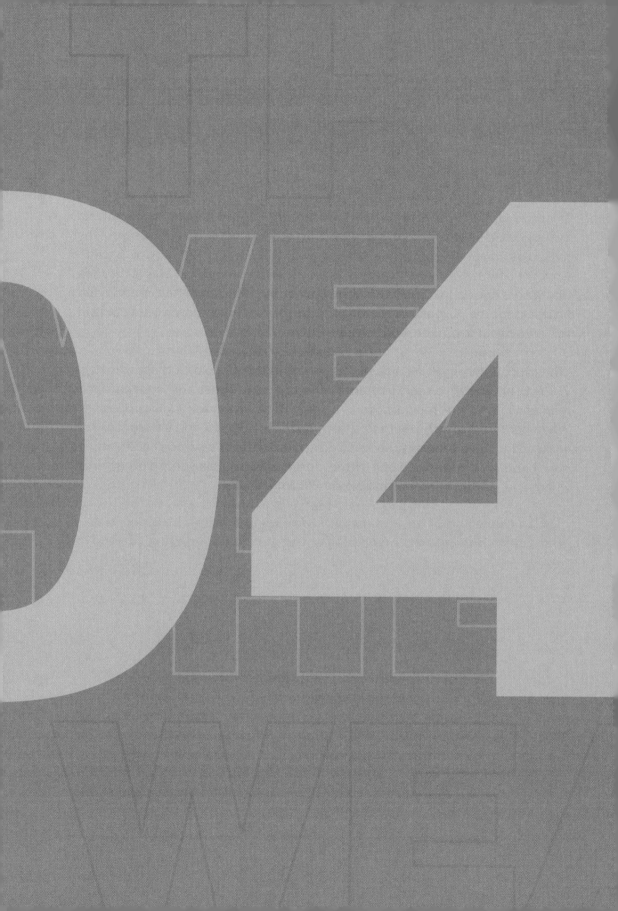

SESSION 4:

WEARING THE RIGHT THING

GRAVE CLOTHES
ARE ANYTHING
THAT HOLD YOU
BACK FROM
EVERYTHING
THAT GOD HAS
FOR YOU.

WATCH GUIDE

Key Scripture:

Therefore, put to death what belongs to your earthly nature (Col. 3:5a).

NOTES

GREAT QUOTE

KEY POINTS

GROUP DISCUSSION

ICEBREAKER

Write pairs of items on individual sticky notes like the following examples: wedding dress/bride, cap and gown/graduation, swimsuit/beach, shoulder pads/football field, coat/winter. Then stick one half of the pair on one student's forehead and the other on another. Don't let them see what their sticky note says. Have them mingle around the room asking each other yes or no questions to figure out what their sticky note says while trying to find their match.

DEBRIEF: Each of these pairs clearly go together and are appropriate for the situation. You don't wear a cap and gown to a wedding. Have you ever shown up somewhere wearing the wrong thing? As Christians, we need to be "wearing" the right thing, and we can't live the new life God has for us if we are still bound in the dressings of our old lives.

RECAP

In John 11:38-44, we see the culmination of Jesus's miraculous acts when Lazarus emerges from the grave after being dead for four days. In calling him back to life, Jesus displayed His power over sickness, disease, and death. However, Lazarus emerged from the darkness of the tomb still wrapped in his grave clothes. Even though he was alive, he still looked and smelled dead. Remember: Grave clothes can represent anything that holds you back from everything God has for you.

GROUP DISCUSSION

All throughout the New Testament we see imagery around believers taking off the old life and putting on the new one. The apostle Paul spends a lot of time talking about this concept. For the next two sessions, we will spend time studying Colossians 3 so that we can identify the grave clothes in our own lives in the hope that we can throw them off and live in freedom and fullness.

ASK A STUDENT TO READ COLOSSIANS 3:1-11.

Notice first that this passage of Scripture is addressed to believers. It is specifically written to those who have been raised with Christ. It is directed to those who have experienced His resurrection power. And for them, Paul described how we live in light of the fact that Jesus has called us from the grave.

**QUESTION: What is his first instruction to believers? Seek
_____ _____ _____(v. 1). What do you think
that means?**

He explained that those who have been raised to life should no longer be focused on the temporary things of this world but must instead fix their eyes on Jesus. If we are alive in Christ, our perspective must change, our mentality must change, everything must change! There is a different way of living for those who have been brought back to life. Paul wanted his audience to understand that God had more in store for them. This relationship with God goes beyond just receiving new life. If the new is alive, what must happen to the old?

Colossians 3:5 says to "_____ _____ _____ your earthly nature."

Paul said to put the old life to death. Kill the old patterns, the old ways, the old behaviors, the old ways of thinking. Put to death anything and everything that stands in the way of you walking in the new life that God has given to you! Take off your grave clothes. Paul gave a list of things we must "put to death."

Read back over Colossians 3:5-10. List what Paul said to put to death:

1. _____   2. _____

3. _____   4. _____

5. _____   6. _____

7. _____   8. _____

9. _____   10. _____

11. _____   12. _____

Ouch. Anyone feeling convicted? First of all, remember that according to Scripture it is the kindness of God that leads us to repentance (Rom. 2:4). This means that it is a good thing when we feel conviction and turn from our sin. Secondly, understand that this is not actually an exhaustive list. Paul is not saying that these are the only things we will have to remove. There are plenty of other grave clothes which might be binding us. It can be unhealthy relationships, addiction, self-harm, suicidal ideation, or any number of other things. God wants you to be free from all of that. Let's look more closely at two of the things Paul listed because they are things so many people struggle with today.

Sexual immorality is the first grave clothes we are going to tackle. Our English phrase is translated from the original Greek *porneia* (πορνεία).[1] You might recognize that the word "pornography" has its origins here. This word describes any sexually related activity outside of God's design. It is important to understand how broad this term is because it could include anything from visiting the wrong websites, to consuming inappropriate TikTok videos, to having sex before or outside of marriage, and much more. Paul's inclusion of impurity and lust means that this challenge of sexual immorality extends even to our thought life.

Our next area of common grave clothes is idolatry. Idolatry is simply the worship of something other than God. An idol is anything or anyone we put in God's place. One of the clearest examples we see in Scripture is in the story of Moses and the Israelites in the book of Exodus. God raised up Moses to lead the people out of slavery in Egypt and into the promised land. In the third month after the people of Israel left Egypt, they came to Mt. Sinai. While they were there, Moses went up to the top of the mountain to speak with God (see Ex. 24). The people began to notice how long Moses had been gone, and they grew impatient in their waiting. So the people gathered around Aaron, Moses's brother and right-hand man, and pleaded with him:

"Come on," they said, "make us some gods who can lead us.
We don't know what happened to this fellow Moses, who brought
us here from the land of Egypt." So Aaron said, "Take the gold
rings from the ears of your wives and sons and daughters,
and bring them to me." All the people took the gold rings from
their ears and brought them to Aaron. Then Aaron took the gold,
melted it down, and molded it into the shape of a calf.
When the people saw it, they exclaimed, "O Israel, these are
the gods who brought you out of the land of Egypt!"
Exodus 32:1–4, NLT

Wait, what? This seems a bit crazy. After all that God had done for them, after all that they had seen Him do, they choose instead to worship a powerless sculpture made from their own jewelry? Though the actions of the Israelites may seem surprising to us, the Lord knows the tendencies of the human heart. He knows our inclination to put other things in His place. That's why the first two commandments He gave to His people were (1) to have no other gods and (2) not to make idols. Our circumstances may be different from the Israelites, but our story is often the same. God shows Himself faithful to us time and time again and still so often we fail to place our faith in Him alone. We turn to lesser gods. You may not bow down to worship a golden statue, but the human heart can make an idol out of almost anything. If we're honest, we may step back and realize that we idolize a relationship, comfort, recognition, success, money, status, or any number of things. We cannot live a free and full life until we have no other gods or idols in our lives.

> ⑦ **QUESTION: How do you wear the right thing and get rid of the grave clothes keeping you from who God wants you to be?**

CLOSING PRAYER: Lord, we offer our idols and lesser gods up to You. Put to death everything in us that is the old self and let the new person You are creating us to be shine brightly for You. Amen.

What Makes God Angry?

? **What is the first thing that comes to your mind when you think about God?**

A.W. Tozer once wrote, "What comes into our minds when we think about God is the most important thing about us."[2] His intention was to communicate that our view of God determines everything about us. All of our decisions, all of our interactions, and all of our thoughts will be dramatically affected by what we think about God. If you think God is loving, and merciful, and gracious, and kind, then that will impact your life. If you think God is hateful, or merciless, or angry, then that will also impact your life.

Colossians 3 helps us to understand the sin we need to take off, and the things of God that we need to put on. Colossians 3:6 (NLT) says, "Because of these sins, the anger of God is coming." Notice where God's anger is directed—sin. God hates sin. Many often throw that statement around without ever considering why God hates sin.

? **Why does God hate sin?**

There are two primary reasons. The first is because sin is the opposite of who God is. God's character is completely pure and holy. His nature is blameless and perfect. God can do no wrong. In Him there is no evil. He is good and He does good. Remember the definition of sin from Romans 3:23? It is falling short of God's standards. God commands us to be holy as He is holy. When we pursue holiness, we become more like God. When we pursue sin, we move away from God's character and likeness. God longs for us to be like Him!

The second reason, I believe, that God hates sin is because it destroys what He loves most: you and me. Sin will not produce in our lives any of the things God desires for us. It is the opposite of what He longs to see in our lives. Why? Because God knows the consequences of our sins. He knows how it will destroy our perspectives, our relationships, and ultimately our lives.

(?) **What has been your view of sin up to this point in your life?**

Colossians 1:15 describes Jesus as the "image of the invisible God." That is to say the clearest picture we have of the heart, character, and nature of God is in the person and work of Jesus. Colossians 1:19 (ESV) tells us that in Christ "the fullness of God was pleased to dwell." If you want to see God, you only need to look at Jesus. If you want to know God, you need only encounter Jesus. Jesus, who is God, loved us enough to lay down His life for us. John 15:13 says, "No one has greater love than this: to lay down his life for his friends." Romans 5:8 reminds us that God demonstrated his own love for us in this: "But God proves his own love for us in that while we were still sinners, Christ died for us." Christ died so that we might live. God hates sin because it is killing us. But God desires for us to have an abundant life (John 10:10).

(?) **Can you think of a time when you hated something because of the effect it had on people you care about? Describe it.**

PRAY: Lord Jesus, thank You for loving me enough to lay down Your life for me. Help me to hate sin the way You do and to love the way You love. Amen.

What Should Direct Our Decisions?

And let the peace of Christ, to which you were also called in one body, rule your hearts. And be thankful. Let the word of Christ dwell richly among you, in all wisdom teaching and admonishing one another through psalms, hymns, and spiritual songs, singing to God with gratitude in your hearts. And whatever you do, in word or in deed, do everything in the name of the Lord Jesus, giving thanks to God the Father through him.
Colossians 3:15–17

Paul packed a lot of truth into a few short verses. Here he explained how we make decisions in the new life by pointing out a few things that ought to guide our thinking as we seek to honor God in all we do. I want to explore three of those together.

The first is the peace of Christ. Colossians 3:15 says, "And let the peace of Christ, to which you were also called in one body, rule your hearts. And be thankful." At the forefront of our thinking should be whether our actions contribute to peace. Many of us are anxious, stressed, worried, and overwhelmed. People are struggling with depression at an all-time high rate. We desperately need the peace of Christ, which surpasses all understanding, to rule in our hearts. But the struggle for peace is not just internal. Peace is a rare thing in our world. It seems that everywhere we look there is tension, disunity, injustice, violence, and hatred. But we desperately need the peace of Christ to rule and reign in the world. So we must ask ourselves at every opportunity, does my decision promote peace or reject it?

(?) **How can you be one who promotes peace?**

The second is the Word of Christ. Colossians 3:16 says, "Let the word of Christ dwell richly among you, in all wisdom teaching and admonishing one another through psalms, hymns, and spiritual songs, singing to God with gratitude in your hearts." Does the Word of Christ dwell in you richly? Does it inform your thinking? Are we using God's Word, as revealed to us in the Scriptures, to inform our perspectives, thoughts, and decisions? Have we made God's Word our standard for living? Do we care more about what the Word says than about what the world says? If we allow God's Word to guide our decisions, we will always make the right choice. According to Psalm 119:105 (KJV), His Word is a "lamp unto my feet, and a light unto my path." This means the Word of God illuminates the direction we should go and the decisions we should make.

(?) **How has God's Word guided your path up to this point in your life?**

The third is the name of Christ. Colossians 3:17 says, "And whatever you do, in word or in deed, do everything in the name of the Lord Jesus, giving thanks to God the Father through him." This ought to be the guiding principle for any decision or action in our lives: Do everything in the name of the Lord Jesus as His representative, as His ambassador, as His image-bearer. If I take into consideration that my every thought, word, and action is an opportunity to reflect Christ to the world around me, it ought to change the way I live. Paul said something similar in 1 Corinthians 10:31, "So, whether you eat or drink, or whatever you do, do everything for the glory of God." Every reaction, every conversation, every relationship, every video we watch or post, every joke we make, all the work that we do, it should all be done in the name of Jesus.

(?) **How can you represent the name of Jesus well?**

PRAY: Lord Jesus, help me to be an agent of peace. Help me to be a student of Your Word. Help me to be an representative of Your name. Amen.

Life Graph

Today is a little different; it is more of an activity than a devotion. A few years ago, I was challenged to do a life graph. I had never heard of that before, and I wasn't very good with graphs. I learned, however, that it is a simple tool that can be used to process some of the most significant events of our lives. When presented to others, it can be a incredible way of communicating a lot about yourself in a short amount of time. Today you are going to make a life graph. Don't worry, I've included mine as an example below. Here's how to do it:

Step 1: Carefully list what you think are the 10-15 most impactful and significant events of your life. There should be a mix of both positive and negative experiences.

Step 2: Draw a line graph like the one you see below. The horizontal axis should list the years of your life from birth to now. The vertical axis should basically move from happiest at the top to saddest at the bottom.

Step 3: Plot the events that you have listed out on the life graph.

Step 4: Connect the dots chronologically to chart the ups and downs of your life.

Step 5: Take some time to process where each event landed and why.

Step 6: Bring this life graph to your next session and be prepared to share the events on this graph during the first few minutes.

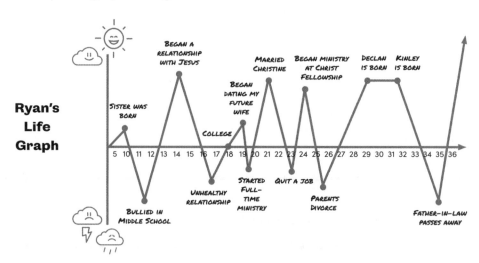

Ryan's Life Graph

Step 1: List 10-15 of the most impactful/significant events of your life.

Steps 2-3: Draw your graph below and plot out the significant events you listed in Step 1.

Step 4: Connect the dots.

Step 5: Process.

(?) **What events went on the happy side? Why?**

(?) **What events went on the sad side? Why?**

PRAY: Through the ups and the downs of my life, Lord Jesus, I trust You! Amen.

SESSION 5:

PUT ON LOVE

IF THERE IS
A UNIFORM FOR
A CHRISTIAN,
IT IS LOVE.

WATCH GUIDE

> **Key Scripture:**
>
> Above all, put on love, which is the perfect bond of unity (Col. 3:14).

NOTES

GREAT QUOTE

KEY POINTS

GROUP DISCUSSION

ICEBREAKER

Ask students to share the life graphs they prepared during Day 3 of their personal study.

RECAP

Last week, we shifted our focus from John 11 to Colossians 3 as we considered the old things that need to come off in favor of the new that God has for us.

GROUP DISCUSSION

Direct students to find Colossians 3:11 in their Bibles and ask the following questions:

What divide was Paul addressing by saying there is no longer Greek and Jew? _____.

What divide was Paul addressing by saying there is no longer circumcision and uncircumcision? _____.

What divide was Paul addressing by saying there is no longer barbarian and Scythian? _____.

What divide was Paul addressing by saying there is no longer slave and free? _____.

1) Nationality, 2) Former religions, 3) Ethnicities, 4) Social and economic class

In his book, *Moments 'til Midnight*, Brent Crowe wrote:

Paul demonstrates how being made new doesn't create new division but rather causes old division to disappear. . . . The new life heaven has made possible causes all other distinguishing characteristics to take a back seat. I think we can all agree that we live in a world of distinctions and division: republican/democrat, hipster/ skater, athlete/mathlete, white/

black, American/Iranian, Baptist/Methodist. But God bids you to come to Jesus and start a journey. Then we can discover something beautiful and mesmerizing, something no other movement has ever accomplished: in Jesus there is no distinction because in Jesus distinctions disappear.[1]

> **? QUESTION: What are some things that people allow to divide them right now? What are some things we allow to create divide between ourselves and others?**

ACTIVITY

ASK A VOLUNTEER TO READ COLOSSIANS 3:12-17.

After painting this picture of division and divide dissolving in Jesus, Paul began to describe the wardrobe of grace that you and I are called to wear as followers of Jesus. What does he tell us to put on?

1. _____.

2. _____.

3. _____.

4. _____.

5. _____.

6. _____.

7. _____.

8. _____.

> **? QUESTION: How do you think most people define the word "love"? How would you define love? Do you think that definition fits what Paul is talking about here?**

What is love? To be honest, the English language falls a little short here, because we just have one word for love: love. So I love my wife, and I love hot Cheetos. I don't love them the same, but since I only have one option in using the word "love," I'm going to maintain that I love them both. The Bible is different. The New Testament was written primarily in Greek, and the Greek language has a lot more words that are used to express different types of love. There are four primary words for love in the Greek language. The first three have to do with friendship, parenting, or family, including one which describes the type of love reserved only for marriage. But *agape*, the fourth word, is the term used in this passage. It is the word most often used in the New Testament to describe God's kind of love.

ACTIVITY

Look up these verses to better understand what agape love is all about: John 15:13; Romans 5:8; Romans 8:39; 1 John 3:16.

The cross of Jesus Christ is the greatest demonstration of love the world has ever seen. Why? Because it was sacrificial, the recipients of this act of love are undeserving, and because God loved us when we did not or could not love Him. If we don't understand the cross, we don't understand love. It is how we know love at all. We love because God has loved us, and we demonstrate love in the same manner that Christ has demonstrated love toward us.

> **So now I am giving you a new commandment: Love each other.**
> **Just as I have loved you, you should love each other.**
> John 13:34, NLT

Guess what word is used three times in this verse. Agape. We are commanded to love others with the same kind of love that God has demonstrated for us in Christ. We are to love people sacrificially and unconditionally. Agape can be understood as a love that is not limited by conditions. This is not an "I will love you if…" kind of love. I will love you if you love me. I will love you if it benefits me. I will love you if you help me. I will love you if you walk like, talk like, think like, vote like me. This is an "I will love you even if…" kind of love. I will love you *even if* you don't love me. I will love you *even if* it doesn't benefit me. I will love *even if* you don't help me. I will love you *even if* you don't walk like, talk like, think like, vote like me. It is a love without conditions or prerequisites.

I get a glimpse of this kind of love every summer through the students at my church. Each year, we take a group of students to an incredible community in South Florida where we have the privilege to love and serve some beautiful people. I watch students scrub dirty desks, mop gritty floors, and paint school classrooms and hallways. I watch young ladies swing jump ropes for hours so the kids who come to play will know that they are loved. I watch students who have brought their own money pray and ask the Holy Spirit to lead them to a person in need who they can bless in some way. They visit the sick, sit with the lonely, deliver meals to the hungry, and pray for the broken-hearted. I can close my eyes and picture a young woman from our church who took off her own shoes to give as a gift in Jesus's name after meeting a person without any of their own. It is possible for each and every one of us to find ways to display unconditional, sacrificial love—agape—to those around us. This is in part what Jesus intended to communicate in His response to the question, "Teacher, which command in the law is the greatest?"

> *He said to him, "Love the Lord your God with all your heart, with all your soul, and with all your mind. This is the greatest and most important command. The second is like it: Love your neighbor as yourself. All the Law and the Prophets depend on these two commands."*
> Matthew 22:36–40

You will be known for what you wear. I am not talking about the shirt on your back or the shoes on your feet. I am saying that if you and I clothe ourselves in agape, the love that has been demonstrated for us in Christ, then the world will know what true love looks like through us. I think of John 13:35, "By this everyone will know that you are my disciples, if you love one another." If the love of God we have received in Jesus doesn't change the way we love other people, then we have completely missed the point.

⑦ QUESTION: How is God calling you to live differently this week?

CLOSING PRAYER: Lord Jesus, help me be unbound—to take off the old and put on love. Teach me to love others as You have loved me. Help me to give an "even if" kind of love. Amen.

You Are Chosen

"Therefore, as God's chosen ones, holy and dearly loved . . ."
Colossians 3:12a

These few words are vital to living the new life Jesus is calling us to. Before Paul listed what we are to do in the second half of Colossians 3:12, he reminded us of who we are. Who we are determines what we do. Paul used these words to speak identity over his audience. He reminded us that in Jesus, we are chosen, holy, and dearly loved.

It feels good to be chosen, doesn't it? When you get picked for the team, selected for the scholarship, honored, or recognized as special, it feels good. Not surprisingly, it hurts when we don't get picked, make the cut, or feel unwanted. How amazing it is to know that you were not only handcrafted by the Creator of the universe, but you were also chosen by Him? He looked across the landscape of history and said, "I want that one."

 Other than Colossians 3:12, what other verse(s) in the Bible help you know that God has chosen you? If you can't think of any, use the concordance in the back of many Bibles to explore what other verses say.

In 2004, Eli Manning entered the NFL draft. He was under a lot of pressure because six years earlier his brother, Peyton, was selected as the first overall pick in the draft by the Indianapolis Colts. Eli had an incredible college football career at Ole Miss and, like his brother, was slated to be the number one overall pick. The top pick that year belonged to the (then) San Diego Chargers (now based in Los Angeles). Before the draft, Eli made it known that if the Chargers selected him, he would not play for the team. He had his heart set on something else; he had always wanted to play for the New York Giants, who would be the fourth team to select a player. Eventually, Eli was chosen as the first overall pick by the San Diego Chargers. He was officially on the team for a grand total of forty-five minutes before he was traded to—you guessed it—the New York Giants.[2]

Here's the deal, God has already picked you. He has chosen you. You just need to decide if you are willing to play for His team. You can wear any jersey you want, but God longs to have you on His team! You are His number one draft pick. He has done everything necessary to get you, but you must decide if you will embrace the fact that you have been chosen and play for His team.

This is why Paul reminded his audience of who they were before he told them what to do. The fact that we have been handpicked by the Creator of the universe should make us want to identify with Him and put on the uniform Paul described in the rest of Colossians 3:12. When you know you are chosen, it's easier to put on humility, gentleness, patience, forgiveness, and love.

 **Who's team are you on? How do people know?**

PRAY: Lord Jesus, thank You for choosing me. Thank You for wanting me. Help me to understand who I am in You so that I can clearly represent You to those around me. Amen.

You Are Holy

This week, we are considering the three words Paul used to describe what unbound followers of Jesus look like: "chosen, holy, and dearly loved" (Col. 3:12). Paul desired for Christians to understand their identity in Jesus. He believed that understanding this identity would shape a believer's life and actions. Throughout Scripture, God's people are described as holy and called to live a life of holiness.

ACTIVITY: Look up and summarize the following verses about holiness:

Leviticus 20:26

Romans 12:1

Ephesians 1:4

Hebrews 12:14

1 Peter 1:15-16

I think to understand what it means to be holy, it is helpful to look at the story of the Israelites in Exodus 14. At that time, God's people had been enslaved in Egypt for over 400 years. The Lord called a man named Moses and raised him up to be the one to finally set these people free. It's pretty dramatic; you should read it. One of the first obstacles to their freedom was crossing the Red Sea with no boats. If that wasn't enough, Pharaoh changed his mind about letting them go and sent his army to capture them. When the Israelites reached the Red Sea, God literally split the waters and gave His people dry ground to walk across. After they had passed through, the waters crashed back down and destroyed Pharaoh's entire army.

? **When was a time in your life where God clearly provided for your needs?**

After this, the children of Israel walked straight into the promised land and everyone lived happily ever after. The end. Right?

Actually, no. The Israelite people wandered around in the desert for forty years. Can you imagine? Moving from place to place, setting up tents, carrying the few possessions they had with them at all times. God had to provide them with literal bread from heaven, so they would not starve on the journey. So why the wandering? Why the desert? God got them out of slavery, but it would take some time before the slavery was out of them. He delivered them from Egypt— He was taking them to the promised land, but God still had some work to do in the wilderness. If you read the story, you will see the people weren't grateful for their freedom. They were frustrated. They were complaining. At one point, they literally considered going back to Egypt to become slaves again. It's actually in this season that God gave the Ten Commandments. Not as a list of rules or regulations. Not as limitations. Rather, He gives the Ten Commandments to His people as a description of what they ought to look like.

It is as if God was saying, "I want you to look different than where you came from." These people had been enslaved for over 400 years. They had forgotten nearly everything about who they were. God was saying "You are not Egyptians; you are mine. Here is what it looks like to be mine." He also knew the land He was sending them to had people He didn't want them to look like either. He wanted them to look like His people. It was like He was saying, "So, let's just stay out here in the desert until we figure this out." Why? Because the people of God look different than everyone else. God's people are set apart. That is what it means to be holy.

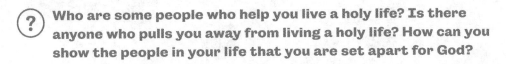 **Who are some people who help you live a holy life? Is there anyone who pulls you away from living a holy life? How can you show the people in your life that you are set apart for God?**

PRAY: God, help me to be more like You. Help me to be holy as You are holy. Help me to look different than the world around me today. Amen.

You Are Dearly Loved

In 1964, a sixteen-year-old kid named Frank stood in a mostly empty court room and looked up at a judge that he could barely see over the bench. In that moment, he had to make a very important decision. At sixteen, most people are looking forward to getting their driver's license, going out with their friends, and having personal freedom. But Frank's parents were getting divorced, and the judge was asking him who he wanted to live with. Frank realized in that moment that he didn't really want to live with his mom or dad. So right then and there, he made up his mind to run away. That night, Frank took out his license and changed his age from sixteen to twenty-six. That act began a five-year journey of forgery and fraud that took Frank to twenty-six countries and all fifty U.S. states. Frank would move from place to place assuming various identities. By the time he was done, he had pretended to be a college professor, an airline pilot, a lawyer, and a doctor, all while cashing over 2.5 million dollars in fraudulent checks. He was finally caught and went to prison. Maybe you've heard the story before, but at the time when Frank committed these crimes, no one had ever heard of this. No one had even thought it. Frank had an identity problem. He didn't know who he was. And that identity problem caused all kinds of trouble for Frank. The truth is that we too have an identify problem. We don't know who we really are in Christ. We don't understand our true identity. And that will cause all kinds of trouble for us.

(?) In one sentence, what would you say is your identity?

That is why Paul took time in Colossians 3:12 to remind Christians who they are before telling them what to do. Who we are determines what we do. Our identity will determine our activity. So Paul reminded us that in Christ, we are chosen, we are holy, and we are dearly loved.

I just want to remind you today that you are dearly loved by the God of the universe. Nothing and no one can take that away from you. That is who you are. Paul asked a question about this in Romans 8:35, "Who can separate us from the love of Christ? Can affliction or distress or persecution or famine or nakedness or danger or sword?" It's almost rhetorical. It's almost as if we should know the answer, but just in case we don't, he reminded us.

> *No, in all these things we are more than conquerors*
> *through him who loved us. For I am persuaded that*
> *neither death nor life, nor angels nor rulers, nor things*
> *present nor things to come, nor powers, nor height nor depth,*
> *nor any other created thing will be able to separate us from the*
> *love of God that is in Christ Jesus our Lord.*
> Romans 8:37–39.

Nothing can separate you from the love of God in Christ. You are dearly loved. Do not forget it. Don't allow anyone to take that truth from you. Walk in the confidence of who God has created you and called you to be. You have all the love you will ever need in Him.

(?) **What things in your life best remind you of this truth? What things discourage you from this truth?**

In Ephesians, Paul prayed that Christians would somehow be able to understand the love that God has for them in Jesus. He wrote, "May [you] have the power, together with all the Lord's holy people, to grasp how wide and long and high and deep is the love of Christ, and to know this love that surpasses knowledge—that you may be filled to the measure of all the fullness of God" (Eph. 3:18-19, NIV).

God is not hiding His love from you. It's written on every page of Scripture and most clearly displayed through Jesus. The ability to grasp His love is within reach, but not without wearing the right clothes and taking the old grave clothes off.

PRAY: Lord, help me to understand a little more of Your love for me today, and may everything I do be motivated by who I am in You. Amen.

SESSION 6:

THE STARTING LINE

THIS IS NOT
THE FINISH LINE.
THIS IS
THE STARTING LINE.

WATCH GUIDE

Key Scripture:

Jesus said to them, "Take off the grave clothes and let him go" (John 11:44, NIV).

NOTES

GREAT QUOTE

KEY POINTS

GROUP DISCUSSION

RECAP

In John 11, the culmination of Jesus's miraculous acts occurred when Lazarus emerged from the grave after being dead for four days. In calling him back to life, Jesus displayed His power over sickness, disease, and death. However, Lazarus emerged from the darkness of the tomb not running but still wrapped in his grave clothes. Even though he was alive, he still looked and smelled dead. The same can be true of us. We have to identify our grave clothes—anything that holds us back from everything God has for us. We have to shed the old, dead life and choose to clothe ourselves in the things of God. In doing so, we get a glimpse of the fullness and freedom God has for us. But now what? Now the journey begins.

ICEBREAKER

Ask students to answer these questions:

What is the best trip you've ever been on? Why?

What is the worst trip you've ever been on? Why?

How do you feel about road trips?

DEBRIEF: As we wrap up our study, it is important for you to understand that freedom is a journey. In fact, it's a lot like a road trip. It's not just about the destination. For people who love to take road trips, the journey is an important part of the whole experience. On that journey, there will be some detours you didn't plan on taking, and some parts of the trip will take much longer than expected. There may even be some things that stop you in your tracks.

GROUP DISCUSSION

I remember taking some road trips when our kids were in the wonderful "are we there yet?" phase of life. Don't pretend you didn't do it—we were all once the "are we there yet" kid. The first time my son asked me, "Are we there yet?" I didn't know how to respond. I wanted to reply, "Yes, we are almost there," just so he wouldn't ask again. But I also didn't want to lie to him. So I just started saying, "We are on our way," because regardless of our place on the journey, it was always true. We were always on our way!

If we are honest, sometimes the journey toward freedom and fullness can feel like that. *Are we there yet? Have we arrived?* I raised my hand in church service—Are we there yet? I've been showing up to Bible study for six straight weeks—Are we there yet? I opened up to someone about my struggle—Are we there yet? In all of those instances, you're not there yet. So what's the answer? *You're on your way.* Freedom is not a destination; it is a journey. If you remain committed to pursuing everything God has for you, you will always be on your way. You will be closer to experiencing the life that God has for you than you were when you started. Don't grow weary in doing this. Be steadfast. Be faithful. God has more in store for you.

ACTIVITY

We need people to come alongside us and help us as we are on our way. Look up the following verses that will help you better understand what this looks like. Next to each verse, write out how it is helping you on your way.

Proverbs 17:17 _____

Proverbs 27:17 _____

Romans 12:4-5 _____

Galatians 6:2 _____

Hebrews 10:24-25 _____

We need people who will help us to loose the grave clothes and walk in freedom, because we can't get them off on our own.

PERSONAL QUESTION

Who are your "them"? Take time to write down the names of some of the people that God has put in your life to help you on the journey toward freedom and fullness. It may be helpful to identify at least one person who is farther along on the journey than you are. Maybe a parent or a pastor or a mentor. You should also identify someone who is on the journey with you, running at your same pace, at your side. Maybe a friend, sibling, or someone from this group. We should also identify someone who needs to understand these truths. Who can you help on their freedom journey? Take a moment and answer these questions on your own.

Who is ahead of you? _____

_____

Who is beside you? _____

_____

Who is behind you? _____

_____

The news about what Jesus had done for Lazarus spread quickly. Almost immediately after this miracle, the religious leaders who opposed Jesus started plotting against Him, concerned the message He was preaching and the miracles He was performing might cause them to lose their status and power. I would imagine Lazarus himself never stopped proclaiming the good news of what Jesus had done for him and what He could do for others.

⑦ **QUESTION: Who is someone you've met that is very open and honest about what Jesus has done for them? How can you be more open to sharing your story like they are?**

ASK FOR A VOLUNTEER TO READ JOHN 11:45.

> *Therefore, many of the Jews who came to Mary and saw what [Jesus] did believed in him.*
> John 11:45

In keeping with their custom, many Jews would have gathered around Mary and Martha to mourn the loss of their brother Lazarus. This would have meant there was a crowd of people present on the day when Lazarus was called back from death and out of the tomb. They watched him hobble out of the grave fully alive. They watched the grave clothes being removed. They watched Lazarus walking away from that grave site alive and free. What was the result? They believed in Jesus. They believed He is the Son of God. They believed He is the Messiah. They too believed Jesus is the resurrection and the life.

I believe others will believe in Jesus because of what He has done and is doing in you. I believe people are going to look upon your life, your fullness, and the change in you, and believe in Jesus because of what they have seen happen in you. Remember the point of the whole Gospel of John?

> *But these are written so that you may believe that Jesus is the Messiah, the Son of God, and that by believing you may have life in his name.*
> John 20:31

The whole point is *belief*. The same thing can be said about our lives. God wants to write a beautiful, powerful, miraculous story through our lives, so that people may believe in Jesus, and by believing, have life in His name. This miracle wasn't just for Lazarus but for all who witnessed it. What did they do with their newfound belief in Jesus? They shared it! They told anyone who would listen to them about the resurrection power of Jesus and what He did for Lazarus and what He could do for them.

> *Meanwhile, the crowd, which had been with him when he called Lazarus out of the tomb and raised him from the dead, continued to testify.*
> John 12:17

I love that. They continued to testify about the person and work of Jesus. What about you? Will you continue to testify about what you have seen? Will you continue to testify about what you have experienced? Will you continue to testify about Jesus so others might find life, fullness, and freedom, which only comes from a growing relationship with Jesus Christ?

? QUESTION: What is your next step? Who is it that God is calling you to share your faith with?

Please understand that this isn't the finish line. This is the starting line.

CLOSING PRAYER: Take time to pray over each student by name. Invite students to lay their hands on the shoulder of the person you are praying for. Pray that each of them would live, from this moment on, in the life and freedom that can only be found in a growing relationship with Jesus Christ. Amen.

LEADER GUIDE

LEADER GUIDE

Thank you for your commitment to students—to loving them well and leading them into deeper relationship with God and others. We pray that you will courageously teach the truth no matter what students think. And we pray that students will be unbound from the grave clothes they may still be clinging to.

Pray

Before you meet with your group, pray. Ask God to prepare you to lead this study, and spend time praying specifically for the students in your group before every session. Ask God to prepare students to approach each session's topic with maturity and grace.

Prepare

Don't wing the group sessions; come to group time prepared. Review the Group Discussion and watch the videos before presenting the material to students. Dig in as you preview each session, making notes and marking specific areas of focus for your group. Consider the age, maturity level, and needs of your group before diving into the content.

Reach Out

Encourage students in your group to complete each day of personal study following the group sessions. Throughout the week, follow up with group members. Consider reaching out about a specific prayer request or diving further into a question a student may have been afraid to ask in front of the whole group.

Evaluate and Change

After each session, think about what went well and what might need to change for you to effectively lead the study. If students seem hesitant to open up, consider placing them in smaller groups as they discuss the video and discussion pages together.

Session 1: When Jesus Shows Up

WATCH: Watch the video teaching and encourage students to follow along with the video guide on pages 8-9.

ICEBREAKER: Start off by making sure everyone in the group knows each other. Ask each student to introduce themselves, then begin the icebreaker.

Think of a moment that the students in your group would all be familiar with. Maybe a recent sporting event or story from summer camp that most, if not all, would have experienced. Then ask a student who witnessed the event to explain what happened. After allow another student to detail any differences in what they remember from the first account. If time permits, allow someone who wasn't there to recap what they heard happened. It's probable there will be discrepancies between the eyewitness accounts and the ones who only heard what happened after.

DEBRIEF: The point of this icebreaker is to help students understand that the best perspective comes from those who saw something for themselves.

GROUP DISCUSSION: Use the Group Discussion beginning on page 10 to guide conversation with your group. Don't feel obligated to ask all the questions; use what works best for your group and let the discussion go where it needs to go.

SCRIPTURE: John 11:1-8

KEY TAKEAWAYS:
- John is an eyewitness account of the life of Jesus, so it is trustworthy.
- The story of Lazarus is not just about someone being brought back to life, but about Jesus willingly laying down His life for His friend.
- The seven "I Am" statements Jesus made about Himself were confusing, controversial, and offensive to some because through them He was making it clear He and the Father are one.
- Through raising Lazarus back to life, Jesus revealed there is resurrection power in Him that is available not just in the next life but in this life as well.
- When Jesus shows up, dead things come to life!

CLOSE IN PRAY: Record any prayer requests and follow up with students during the week.

Session 2: Do You Believe?

WATCH: Watch the video teaching and encourage students to follow along with the video guide on pages 22-23.

ICEBREAKER: Play a game called "Do you believe this?" in which students identify whether they believe something to be true or false. If they believe it, direct them to stand. If they do not, ask students to stay seated. Sample questions are found on page 24, and feel free to add more questions if you would like to extend the game.

RECAP: In Session 1, we barely began to scratch the surface of all that God has to teach us through this story in John 11. We listened to and, hopefully, felt the story of Lazarus in a fresh new way. Now that we know the story, we have to ask ourselves if we understand the story. What really is the point of this passage? What does it mean for you and me today? Is this just Lazarus's story, or could it be more?

GROUP DISCUSSION: Use the Group Discussion beginning on page 25 to guide conversation with your group. Don't feel obligated to ask all the questions; use what works best for your group and let the discussion go where it needs to go.

SCRIPTURE: John 11:17-27

KEY TAKEAWAYS:
- Be prepared to share your personal salvation story. Talk about the moment when you came to believe that Jesus is the resurrection and life. Include elements of your life before Jesus and how you've changed since becoming a Christ-follower.
- We must all come to that place of belief and confession like Martha did in John 11:27.
- There may be students in your group who have not placed their faith in Jesus. If this is the case, use the outline on pages 26-27 to help guide you through a conversation with them.
- Allow each person to take a few minutes to tell the story of when they first placed their faith in Jesus.

CLOSE IN PRAY: Record any prayer requests and follow up with students during the week.

Session 3: Grave Clothes

WATCH: Watch the video teaching and encourage students to follow along with the video guide on pages 36-37.

ICEBREAKER: Ask students to get into groups of 2-4 people. Give each group a roll of toilet paper. The goal is to see which group can wrap the roll of toilet paper around one of the students in the group the quickest. Make sure they stay wrapped up when they finish. Once one person from each group is completely wrapped and you have identified the winning group, then have students escape from the toilet paper that binds them as quickly as they can.

RECAP: In the last session we talked about our belief in Jesus and told each other our stories of how we came to faith in Him. Can you imagine the story Lazarus had to tell?

GROUP DISCUSSION: Use the Group Discussion beginning on page 38 to guide conversation with your group. Don't feel obligated to ask all the questions; use what works best for your group and let the discussion go where it needs to go.

SCRIPTURE: John 11:38-44

KEY TAKEAWAYS:
- The grave clothes that bound Lazarus after Jesus called him back from the dead are a perfect picture of how many of us are still bound. Let's go back to Genesis and see why we still cling to our grave clothes.
- Humanity is distinct from the rest of creation. We were made in the image of God. We were given dominion over everything else that God created. And we were built different from every other thing God created (Gen. 1:26-27; 2:7).
- The four words in Genesis 3:1, "Did God really say?" changed the trajectory of history forever.
- Like Eve in Genesis 3:2, many Christians today misquote God because we don't know His Word for ourselves.
- Eve fell for Satan's trick. She ate the fruit and gave some to Adam, and he ate it too. With that act of disobedience, sin and brokenness entered the world.
- The fig leaves Adam and Eve sewed to cover themselves up in Genesis 3:7 were the very first "grave clothes" we see in Scripture. Grave clothes are anything that holds us back from everything God has for us.

CLOSE IN PRAY: Record any prayer requests and follow up with students during the week.

Session 4: Wearing the Right Thing

WATCH: Watch the video teaching and encourage students to follow along with the video guide on pages 50-51.

ICEBREAKER: Write pairs of items on individual sticky notes, and stick one half of the pair on one student's forehead and the other on another. Don't let them see what their sticky note says. Have them mingle around the room asking each other yes or no questions to figure out what their sticky note says while trying to find their match.

DEBRIEF: Each of these pairs clearly go together and are appropriate for the situation. Have you ever shown up somewhere wearing the wrong thing? As Christians we need to be "wearing" the right thing and we can't live the new life God has for us if we are still bound up in the dressings of the old life.

RECAP: In calling Lazarus back to life, Jesus displayed His power over sickness, disease, and death. However, Lazarus emerged from the darkness of the tomb still wrapped in his grave clothes. Even though he was alive, he still looked and smelled dead. Remember: Grave clothes can represent anything that holds you back from everything God has for you.

SCRIPTURE: Colossians 3:1-11

KEY TAKEAWAYS:
- If we are alive in Christ, our perspective must change, our mentality must change, everything must change. There is a different way of living for those who have been brought back to life.
- Put to death anything and everything that stands in the way of you walking in the new life that God has given to you. Take off your grave clothes.
- Remember that according to Scripture, it is the kindness of God that leads us to repentance (Rom. 2:4). This means that it is a good thing when we feel conviction and turn from our sin.

- Sexual impurity and idolatry are two grave clothes we continue to struggle with even after we believe.
- We cannot live an unbound life until we have no other gods or idols in our lives apart from God.

CLOSE IN PRAY: Record any prayer requests and follow up with students during the week.

Session 5: Put on Love

WATCH: Watch the video teaching and encourage students to follow along with the video guide on pages 64-65.

ICEBREAKER: Ask students to share the life graphs they prepared during Day 3 of their personal study in Session 4.

RECAP: Last week, we shifted focus from John 11 to Colossians 3 as we considered the old things that need to come off in favor of the new that God has for us.

SCRIPTURE: Colossians 3:12-17

KEY TAKEAWAYS:
- In Colossians 3:11, Paul demonstrated how being made new doesn't create new divisions but rather causes old divisions to disappear.
- In Colossians 3:12-17, Paul described the wardrobe of grace that you and I are called to wear as followers of Jesus.
- The English language has one word for love, but there are four primary words for love in the Greek language. *Agape* is the word for love used in Colossians 3:12-17. It is the word most often used in the New Testament to describe God's love.
- We are commanded to love others with the same kind of love that God has demonstrated for us in Christ. We are to love people sacrificially and unconditionally.
- It is possible for each and every one of us to find ways to display unconditional, sacrificial love to those around us.
- If the love of God we have received in Jesus doesn't change the way we love other people, then we have completely missed the point.

CLOSE IN PRAY: Record any prayer requests and follow up with students during the week.

Session 6: The Starting Line

WATCH: Watch the video teaching and encourage students to follow along with the video guide on pages 78-79.

RECAP: In John 11, the culmination of Jesus's miraculous acts occurred when Lazarus emerged from the grave after being dead for four days. In calling him back to life, Jesus displayed His power over sickness, disease, and death. However, Lazarus emerged from the darkness of the tomb not running but still wrapped in his grave clothes. Even though he was alive, he still looked and smelled dead. The same can be true of us. We have to identify our grave clothes—anything that holds us back from everything God has for us. We have to shed the old, dead life and choose to clothe ourselves in the things of God. In doing so, we get a glimpse of the fullness and freedom God has for us. But now what? Now the journey begins.

ICEBREAKER: Ask students to answer these questions:

What is the best trip you've ever been on? Why?

What is the worst trip you've ever been on? Why?

How do you feel about road trips?

DEBRIEF: As we wrap up our study, it is important for you to understand that freedom is a journey. In fact, it's a lot like a road trip. It's not just about the destination. For people who love to take road trips, the journey is an important part of the whole experience. On your journey, there will be some detours you didn't plan on taking. Some parts of the trip will take much longer than expected. There may even be some things that stop you in your tracks.

SCRIPTURE: John 11:45; John 12:17

KEY TAKEAWAYS:

- Freedom is not a destination; it is a journey. If you remain committed to pursuing everything God has for you, you will always be on your way.
- We need people who will help us loose our grave clothes and walk in freedom, because we can't get them off on our own.
- God wants to write a beautiful, powerful, miraculous story, so that through our lives, people may believe in Jesus, and by believing, have life in His name.
- Will you continue to testify about what you have experienced? Will you continue to testify about Jesus so others might find life, fullness, and freedom, which only comes from a growing relationship with Jesus Christ?
- Belief in Jesus is not the finish line; it's the starting line.

CLOSE IN PRAY: Record any prayer requests and follow up with students during the week.

Notes

Notes

SOURCES

Session 1

1. Kenneth L. Barker and William Kruidnier, "Introduction to the Gospel of John," in *Zondervan NASB Study Bible* (Grand Rapids, MI: Zondervan, 2009), 1513.
2. Jeffrey E. Miller, "I Am Sayings," ed. John D. Barry, et al., *The Lexham Bible Dictionary* (Bellingham, WA: Lexham Press, 2016).
3. Ibid.
4. Lewis A. Drummond, *Spurgeon: Prince of Preachers* (Grand Rapids, MI: Kregel Publications, 1992).
5. Charles H. Spurgeon, *Evening by Evening: Or Readings at Eventide* (New York: Robert Carter, 1869), 318.
6. Arnold G. Fruchtenbaum, "The Three Messianic Miracles," in *The Messianic Bible Study Collection* (Tustin, CA: Ariel Ministries, 1998).
7. Ernst Haenchen, Robert Walter Funk, and Ulrich Busse, *John: A Commentary on the Gospel of John, Hermeneia—A Critical and Historical Commentary on the Bible* (Philadelphia: Fortress Press, 1984), 60.

Session 2

1. Abigail Abrams, "Your Cell Phone Is Ten Times Dirtier Than a Toilet Seat. Here's What to Do About It," *TIME*, August 23, 2017. Available from the internet: https://time.com/4908654/cell-phone-bacteria/.
2. "Great Banyan Tree," *Atlas Obscura*, February 16, 2011. Available from the internet: https://www.atlasobscura.com/places/great-banyan-tree#:~:text=The%20Great%20Banyan%20Tree%20is,is%20known%20as%20Ficus%20benghalensis.
3. John M. Henshaw, "How Many Senses Do We Have?" *John Hopkins University Press*, February 1, 2012. Available from the internet: https://www.press.jhu.edu/newsroom/how-many-senses-do-we-have.
4. Matt Davis, "Juan Pujol Garcia: The WWII Double Agent Who Secretly Controlled the War," *Big Think*, August 23, 2018. Available from the internet: https://bigthink.com/politics-current-affairs/juan-pujol-garcia/.
5. Bruce Milne, *The Message of John: Here Is Your King: With Study Guide, The Bible Speaks Today* (Leicester, England; Downers Grove, IL: InterVarsity Press, 1993), 176.
6. Ibid

Session 3

1. Mary Johnson, "Mary Johnson and Oshea Israel," The Forgiveness Project, [accessed July 1, 2022]. Available from the internet: https://www.theforgivenessproject.com/stories-library/mary-johnson-oshea-israel/.

Session 4

1. Strong's G4202, *Blue Letter Bible*, https://www.blueletterbible.org/lexicon/g4202/kjv/tr/0-1/.
2. A.W. Tozer, *The Knowledge of the Holy* (New York: HarperCollins, 1978), 1.

Session 5

1. Brent Crowe, *Moments 'til Midnight: The Final Thoughts of a Wandering Pilgrim* (Nashville, TN: B&H Books, 2018).
2. Agustin Mojica, "The Charger Made the Best Out of Eli Manning's Draft," Sports Casting, March 19, 2020. Available from the internet: https://www.sportscasting.com/the-chargers-made-lemonade-out-of-lemons-with-eli-mannings-2004-draft/.
3. Frank W. Abagnale, Catch Me If You Can: The True Story of Real Fake (New York: Broadway Books, 1980).

Get the most from your study.

Promotional videos and other leader materials available at lifeway.com/unbound.

In the book of John, we read the miraculous story of Jesus raising Lazarus from the dead. As Jesus called to his friend, Lazarus rose from his grave, breathing, moving—fully alive—yet still bound by the clothes he was buried in. Is it possible that, like Lazarus, we too are still bound in our grave clothes? Held back by fear, or pride, or shame. Wrapped up in sin, or hurt, or anger, or unforgiveness. Grave clothes are anything that hold us back from everything God has for us. This describes many believers today—alive in Christ but still bound.

In this new 6-session study, author Ryan McDermott invites us to shed the old life that has held us back and fully embrace the newness of life that Christ has made possible. Jesus died, not just so that we could have life, but so that we might be unbound and step into a new identity: holy, loved, chosen, and free.

Want to watch the *Unbound* teaching videos when and where it is most convenient? Introducing the Lifeway On Demand app! From your smartphone to your TV, watching videos from Lifeway has never been easier. Visit lifeway.com/unbound or the Lifeway on Demand app to purchase the Unbound teaching videos and hear from author Ryan McDermott.

For more information about Lifeway Students, visit lifeway.com/students.